D1137743

WITHDRAWN

THE
TEENAGE WORRIER'S
CHRISTMAS
SURVIVAL GUIDE

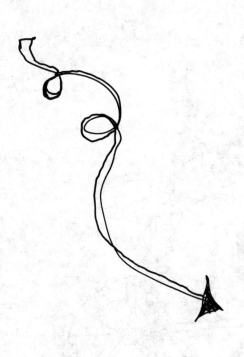

THE TEENAGE WORRIER'S CHRISTMAS SURVIVAL GUIDE

C o l d – (visit casualty with frostbite)

H olly – (visit vet re-holly stuck in pet's paw)

R ibbons – (vet again - strangled gerbil)

I ce – (see 'cold' above)

S NOW – (see 'cold' & 'ice' above)

T urkey – (Panic re-resolution to have nutroast)

M istletoe – (Visit Doc re depression at lack of kissing opportunities)

A ardvark – (Just checking to see you're reading this)

S anta – (Hurl self into abyss at loss of childish innocence)

ROS ASQUITH

Piccadilly Press • London

The right of Ros Asquith to be identified as Author of this work
has been asserted by her in accordance with the Copyright,
Designs and Patents Act 1988.

Phototypeset from author's disk by Piccadilly Press.
Printed and bound in Hungary by Interpress for the
publishers Piccadilly Press Ltd.,
5 Castle Road, London NW1 8PR

A catalogue record for this book is available from the
British Library

ISBN: 1 85340 349 0

Ros Asquith lives in North London. Her cartoon strip, *Doris,*
appears weekly in the *Guardian*. Her other books include:

I WAS A TEENAGE WORRIER
THE TEENAGE WORRIER'S FRIENDS
THE TEENAGE WORRIER'S GUIDE TO LURVE

✧ This book belongs to ✧

AGE...

SEX...

add 2,000 sheets of paper to fit these in.

BIGGEST WORRIES..

SHOE SIZE...

HEIGHT...

WIDTH...

HAIR COLOUR..

EYE DITTO...

NUMBER OF ZITS, PLUKES ETCK.....................

(Do not count eyelashes or measure lips Etck as this only leads to pain and bewilderment)

Mistletoe: stand under this at all times to encourage Romantic encounters

N.B. Do Not feel sorry for the fish. It will make Rover v. happy

Extra Big Stocking: pack with fudge, male models Etck.

Moi: With minimum Christmas accessories.

Rumpled bed
Room-hit-by-tornado
Houselet
Infinitesimal corner of Universe
Cosmos

Dear Teenage Worrier(s),

   "'Tis the season to be Jolly fa-la-la-la-laaaaaaaaa la-la-la-la!"

   And Teenage Worriers everywhere are sunk in glume, festering with worries only deepened by the jocund revelry, the glitter and tinsel that the world displays to mock their solitude (sound of violins, banshees Etck over stark picture of baby seal, gazing mutely, pleadingly at photographer as club descends...). Sorry, got a bit carried away there. Must paint on smile, put on Father Christmas hat and address problems of FESTIVE SEASON.

   One of the V.Biggest Worries, as you put away child-ish things and sob over your old teddy – deciding to keep him in bed with you for just ONE more year (especially since there is no one else to hug, moan, whinge) is how to STOP worrying about spots, the meaning-of-life, the Secret-of-the-Universe, why Nobody Cares Etck and START worrying about that seemingly endless time zone in which you see all those relatives you haven't seen for a year and realise why.

   Christmas, we are told, is a time for the family. For those Teenage Worriers lucky enough to have a family, this may seem something of a contradiction in terms, since those precious morsels of family felicity that have been patiently

7

harvested over the year are usually blown asunder during the festive season, only to be glued back with excruciating slowness — just in time to be shredded anew by the Summer Holiday.

The obligation of parents to buy Christmas tree, curse height of living room, chop tree, sever wrist, wait all night in Casualty, have arm in sling, get pine needle stuck in foot, face quadruple rent arrears on account of present-buying cashflow crisis, get shards of Christmas Tree decoration in other foot, rob bank to pay for turkey, sprain other arm lifting same, set hair alight along with Christmas pudding, collapse V.Drunk in front of embarrassed aunts, offspring Etck leads one to question the true Spirit of the Season — especially since whole family must then spend Jan and Feb in freezing home with all services cut off as a result of seasonal overspend.

Meanwhile visiting relatives are exclaiming.

"Oh, gloves! Lovely. And what an original shape."

"Pillow cases! Gorgeous! And what a lovely shade of beige! Most original."

"A potato peeler! Well, well! How original!"

"What a lovely card darling. Is that the Baby Jesus? No? A tomato? A Christmas Tomato! Well, well! How original."

What does a healthy, normal, Teenage Worrier DO in the face of such revelry? Sulk? Enjoy a small nut roast in the privacy of yr room? Decide to spend day wandering banks of river exchanging hand-painted pebbles and pieces of driftwood with your lurve object? Charming as such notions are, they are likely to lead to loneliness and pining, particularly if yr lurve object has arm round yr best frend as is usually the case with moi...

The above ponderings have led me to put aside my major work on the History-of-Worry, How-to-solve-all-of-life's-problems-while-lying-in-bed-with-big-bag-of-fudge Etck (out next year, please buy) – and pen a V.Quick guide to the problems of Christmas and Beyond, hoping to make a quick buck, I mean help my fellow Worriers in their time of need.

This avidly researched volume will give handy hints on how to BANISH CHRISTMAS GLUME; fill the void of inertia, tedium Etck between Christmas and New Year; and bolster the spirits of Teenage Worriers everywhere to face anew the fresh challenges and invigorating Worries of the Spring ... Summer ... Autumn ... and, er, back to square one.

Please feel free to use it to doodle on, write hit songs in (I only take V.small percentage), make paper chains out of, or even to record yr profoundest fears, hopes, Etck and then check at end of year to see if any have come true. I have, naturellement, put some of my own humble dreams in, which I wld only reveal to you, dear reader.

And now, sadly, I must consider whether to buy a present for the only-one-I-have-ever-lurved, ie, that is, Daniel Hope, who has spurned me twice and yet for whom, occasionally, I still feel a faint throb of tragic yearning. But what could I get him? Please write in and advise me dear reader(s), for I am alone with my pain and who can I turn to but you? Maybe I'll buy something for the only-other-I-have-ever-lurved instead: my faithful cat, Rover. She has stood by me through thin and thick and is V.Easy to please, being quite happy with a ball of wool and ecstatic with a luxury like a rubber mouse.

So, just off to deck the halls with boughs of holly (swallow berry, prick finger, spend day in Casualty dept), go carol singing for charity (earn £2.50 for good cause, get frostbite, spend evening in Accident & Emergency), make Christmas cake (drop egg, skid into little brother Benjy, landing him in Casualty and confirming his fears that all floors are lethal), decorate tree (fall off ladder with Fairy stuck up hooter Etck Etck.)

It must be Christmas.

LURVE,

Letty
Chubb
(aged 15)

LIST WHAT YOU HOPE YOU'LL GET FOR CHRISTMAS HERE

Sample List:

1 Phoenix-of-Doom roller blades that play music of your choice and light up like Piccadilly Circus as you glide.

2 CD Rom computer plus discs that teach you how to Rule world, capture True Lurve Etck.

3 Next year's GCSE exam papers plus answers in all subjects, plus tape of explanations of how you get to those answers in language a three-year-old cld understand, plus essay-writing machine. Lots of kids have these since in Scotland maths answers have already been on the Internet. It is V. Unfair on those of us whose otherwise pushy parents are sadly too principled or too lazy to help us cheat.

4 White horse with wings that shrinks to size suitable for matchbox but grows for you to ride whenever you want.

5 Lifetime's supply of FUDGE.

6 Video camera to get that movie director career rolling.

LIST WHAT YOU EXPECT TO GET HERE:

ie L. Chubb expects: new plimsolls; turquoise and lemon bolero from Granny Chubb (only two sizes too small, since I couldn't bring myself to admit that the orange and purple one she knitted last year was three sizes too small and just mentioned it was a wee bit tight); Video of "Pocahontas" from auntie Vi, who still thinks I am seven but doesn't realise we are sole family in London not to have a video; flea collar for Rover; fiver from my adored father (who will borrow it back on Boxing Day); italic pen writing set (my only mother's attempt to transform my errant script, which more and more resembles a mammoth mating with a dragonfly); bag of fudge.

↑ Pair of Socks (beige)

← strange garment (orange & beige)

NOTHING on tree (sob)

My favourites will be the flea collar (which Rover badly needs) and the bag of fudge as it represents true lurve from Benjy who will have saved one whole lot of tooth fairy money to buy it for me. And will probably only have eaten two or three bits of it himself. Before you take out the violins and kleenex and weep for my lousy list of presents — ask yourself: will yours be any better?

13

What you Expect:	What You Actually Got:
1....................................	1....................................
2....................................	2....................................
3....................................	3....................................
4....................................	4....................................
5....................................	5....................................
6....................................	6....................................
7....................................	7....................................
8....................................	8....................................
9....................................	9....................................
10..................................	10..................................
11..................................	11..................................
12..................................	12..................................
13..................................	13..................................
14..................................	14..................................

LIST PEOPLE YOU NEED TO
BUY/MAKE PRESENTS FOR:

....

....

....

....

....

....

....

....

....

....

....

....

....

N.B. If you have even
HALF as many as this,
You are either V. lucky
or a liar.

CHRISTMAS CARDS:

Relatives are always V. Happy to get homemade card so here are a few humble designs by moi for you to copy. (Not suitable for aged or snooty types.)

Peas on Earth

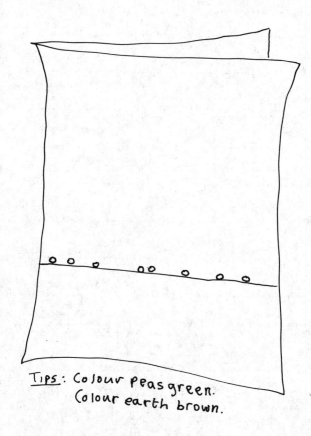

TIPS: Colour peas green.
Colour earth brown.

17

ARE YOU A TRUE CHRISTMAS WORRIER?

Are you Worried about any of the following:
(Tick appropriate box) I am sure I will do REALLY well at <u>this</u> (not like last time).

1 That you might get mugged if you go carol singing?

2 That you might keep carol singing money instead of donating it to Charity?

3 The bang of crackers?

4 Whether turkeys know their fate?

5 Whether roast potatoes know their fate (if VVVV Worried about this seek counselling)?

6 Whether Christmas pud will burn down house as result of adult dousing it with lighter fuel instead of brandy?

7 Whether shard of tinsel will insert itself under your eyelid forcing emergency visit to Eye Hospital in middle of Christmas meal?

8 Whether diminutive relative will choke on contents of cracker?

	VVV Worried	VV Worried	V Worried	Worried	not Worried	HAPPY about
1	☐	☐	☐	☐	☐	☐
2	☐	☐	☐	☐	☐	☐
3	☐	☐	☐	☐	☐	☐
4	☐	☐	☐	☐	☐	☐
5	☐	☐	☐	☐	☐	☐
6	☐	☐	☐	☐	☐	☐
7	☐	☐	☐	☐	☐	☐
8	☐	☐	☐	☐	☐	☐

9 Whether yr sibling knows about Father Christmas?

10 Whether you know about Father Christmas?

11 That you might get a pine needle stuck under your toenail and have to go to hospital on Christmas Eve?

12 Whether "White Christmas" has racist overtones?

13 What the Boy/Gurl of yr dreamz is doing and why haven't they rung/sent card Etck?

14 Whether mince pies are OK for vegetarians?

15 Whether you dare ask for nut roast?

16 Whether adults will get V. Embarrassingly drunk and toast the Queer Old Dean instead of the Dear Old Queen, or be sick on yr sparkling new outfit?

17 Whether yr hooter, cheeks Etck are as red as everyone else's?

18 How to avoid family walk?

19 Whether yr pet will feel left out if not given full nosh plus trimmings?

20 Whether yr pet will feel abandoned if not given Christmas stocking?

	VVV Worried	VV Worried	V Worried	Worried	not Worried	HAPPY about
9	☐	☐	☐	☐	☐	☐
10	☐	☐	☐	☐	☐	☐
11	☐	☐	☐	☐	☐	☐
12	☐	☐	☐	☐	☐	☐
13	☐	☐	☐	☐	☐	☐
14	☐	☐	☐	☐	☐	☐
15	☐	☐	☐	☐	☐	☐
16	☐	☐	☐	☐	☐	☐
17	☐	☐	☐	☐	☐	☐
18	☐	☐	☐	☐	☐	☐
19	☐	☐	☐	☐	☐	☐
20	☐	☐	☐	☐	☐	☐

ANSWERS TO TEENAGE WORRIER QUIZ

Score 10 for VVV Worried; 8 for VV Worried; 6 for V Worried; 4 for Worried; 2 for Not Worried; 0 for HAPPY about.

195-200. You are CORRRECT to be concerned. Ring a Helpline immediately, then go straight to your Doctor or the nearest Casualty Dept.

If only.

155-194. My own score and therefore V.Sane. Others, however, (those without souls Etck) may find this a rather higher level of anxiety than is totally compatible with serenity Etck. To them I say: Tish poo.

114-154. Still a Teenage Worrier -but a borderline case. Almost normal, in fact.

76-113. This is the score I am hoping I will get when I have read, learned and inwardly digested (cough, splutter) all the meaningful info contained in this tome (and in *I Was a Teenage Worrier* and *The Teenage Worrier's Guide to LURVE* puff, plug). I hope you, too, gentle readers, will attain this score. Please let me know if you have.

34-75. CONGRATULATIONS. You have conquered Christmas Worry. You do not need the help of El Chubb. You should be out helping others through this veil of tears Etck. (That should give you something to worry about).

0-33. Porky pies. Check mirror to see if nose is growing.

PIN-UP OF THE MONTH

Father Christmas

← ———— v. soon to be 2,000 someth

Age: One thousand something

Appearance: Right jolly old elf   N.B. must have red hat, white beard Etck.

Pets: Dasher, Vixen Etck

Occupation: A two year old could tell you this, you dimbo

Free time: 364 days a year

Prospects: V.Good job security, own home, transport, long life Etck (none of which things are of the slightest interest to Teenage Worriers, but middle age worriers find V.Fascinating)

Most often heard saying: Ho Ho Ho

Most unlikely to: Diet

↑ Thereby qualifying for El Chubb's AWARD for V. Noble Person.

N.B. Rover has relented and graced me with a PURR. My cup overfloweth.

Look, I started to draw pictures of F.
Christmas on this page. BUT then I thought
you'd prefer a nice frame. In which to
stick a pic of your pin-up. Like your pet
ant, or whoever...

25

TEENAGE WORRIER'S CHRISTMAS DECORATIONS

You may favour simple,
understated approach.

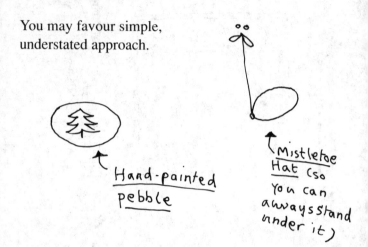

Hand-painted
pebble

Mistletoe
Hat (so
you can
always stand
under it)

Or, more
elaborate confections.

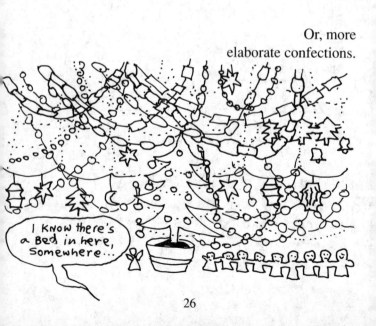

I KNOW there's
a Bed in here,
somewhere...

El Chubb's
TWELVE DAYS of CHRISTMAS

This is a fine old song you have probably heard at Christmas time ever since you were an ickle baba, mewling and puking in your mother's arms Etck. But, romantic though it is, time has marched on, trampling many of the subtle nuances of the original, so that the swain's gifts to his true lurve seem more of a lumber than a luxury... El Chubb takes a look (remember, the opening words of the song are "On the First day of Christmas my true love gave to me..." and then proceeds up to the twelfth day whereupon swain lists vast swathe of offerings...)

Twelve Lords a Leaping...hmmmm. Do you REALLY want twelve Octogenarian peers galloping out of the House of Lords and pogo-ing about in your kitchen? NB I am NOT being ageist, as you know my favourite person in the Universe is Granny Chubb, and I would much prefer her to debate issues of National Importance than the handful of Lords a Sleeping that you occasionally glimpse on TV when the set's working.

Eleven Ladies dancing. Would these be ballroom dancers of the kind that sew on a happy face along with their sequins? Or temptresses with castanets and a rose clamped between their choppers? (I've often worried, as I expect, dear reader, have you – whether they get thorns in their gums. And, if so, if they're allowed to gavotte off stage into the arms of a waiting dentist or whether the show must go on...). Maybe you cld choose a chorus of cygnets in tutus allowing you to be dying swan Etck although I fear in the case of moi it would be the only swan to transform into an Ugly Duckling.

Ten Pipers Piping. I quite fancy a bunch of burly pipers swirling kilts as I have Scottish blood strong in my veins on my adored father's side of the family.

Nine Drummers Drumming. Aaarg (see infant musicians above). On le autre main (as we say in France) this could be a whole stageful of cool jazz and rock drummers complete with congas, kettle drums, cymbals, high hats, low hats, (you can see I've been researching in the rhythm section) in which case er, yes please, please Mr Postman I'll accept this one.

Eight Maids a Milking. Be serious. You want a hallway full of cows?

Seven Swans ... Oh, you all know what comes next. Move on, speedily and infinitely more interestingly to:

NB Quick reminder: 6 Geese a-laying, 5 GO-OLD RINGS, 4 colly birds, 3 French hens, 2 turtle doves or is it 'calling birds'?

El Chubb's (affordable) version for the twenty-first century swain:

On the twelfth day of Christmas my True Love gave to meeeeeeeeeeeeeeeeeeee

Twelve chords a cheeping

(pref played on troubador's mandolin – but electric guitar will do)

Eleven shades for glancing

(I'm always losing sunglasses, so V. large supply will keep me looking kool all Summer)

Ten types of typing

(i.e. he could type: my essays, projects, poems, bukes, lurve letters, letters to Agony Aunts, thank-you letters, and still have three kinds of type left over with which to send me HIS lurve letters, poems Etck. This wld prevent me writing everything out in long-hand since my only parents are too mean to buy me a word processor and my adored father will not let me near his in case I lose the page of his long-awaited novel. Eeek)

Nine plumbers plumming

(not romantic, I know, but we need constant supply in our house to fend off worst effects of my father's DIY, as readers of my other humble tomes will no doubt be aware. However, happy to accept Drummers Drumming, see original above, or strummers strumming as long as V.Handsome guitarists serenading moi)

Eight blades a-hulking

(blades as in dashing romantic young swains. V.Hulky ones pleease. NOT called Daniel Hope)

Seven dons a-hymning

(Dons as in University professors, not Donald Duck, stupid. And they would be hymning my praises, naturellement)

Six Greeks a-swaying

(Greek God look-a-likes, swaying in soft breezes as they stroke their, ahem, instruments)

FIVE G-OLD RINGS

(I'll keep these, thank you – not that I am mercenary, just because I recognise that they are objects of great natural beauty dug from Mother Earth, yawn)

Four scalding words

("Letty, I love you" muttered in simmering tones)

Three French glens

(small gladey dells just outside Paris in which to con-
sume – sorry, consummate – our passion)

Two Turtle Doves

Am accepting these also, as symbol of true lurve.

**AND A HEART-BRIDGE THAT SPANS FROM
HIM TO MEEEEEEEEEE**

(If this makes you reach for sick bag, then think of a
better rhyme. Answers on a postcard. The winner will
get one free copy of each of my other bukes. Runner up
to get two free copies, haha yeeech)

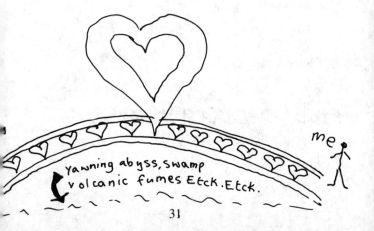

In fact, in un-romantic nineties I am more likely to get following list

12 Wards a-weeping
(NHS on blink)

11 Jades a-chancing
(all of them after my True Lurve)

10 Snipers sniping

9 Bummers bumming

8 Aides a-skulking

7 Cons for slimming

6 Police a-baying

FIVE O-OLD THINGS
(Last year's presents recycled)

Glume
Dume
Despond
Writhe
in eternity
Etck

4 Galling words
("Letty, it's all over" or, if you prefer:"It's all over Letty" which could apply to spilt soup, vomit Etck)

3 Entrenched wens
(NB wen is a cyst on head, which is yet another thing I now have to add to my lengthening list of worries)

2 Hearty shoves

AND A CARTRIDGE
TO SHOW THAT
I AM FREEEEEEEEEEEEE

(Unless gun laws changed soon we will all be walking about with automatic pistols Etck. Arg.)

On which note of glume and despond, I end my little survey of one of our most enduring popular songs.

Signed

Professor L. Chubb.
(University of Ennui.)

COUNTDOWN TO CHRISTMAS

Although, doubtless, you will have received this humble tome on Christmas Day, you may be one of those Teenage Worriers who snuck out and bought it for themselves and therefore will be delighted to have El Chubb's guidelines for the month leading up to the Big Day. Also V.Useful to compare and contrast with yr own experiences Etck. Or to use next year, blah blah. So, here goes (fanfare):

WEEK ONE Dec 1-7

Tell adored parents you are are too old for Advent Calendar and persuade them —in true Spirit of Christmas— to give yours to little girl next door who is always crying. Feel glow of pride.

Proceed to jealously watch younger sibling open Advent calendar covered in frosty sparkles with merrily chortling reindeer Etck. Notice that inside is not just a picture of a wooden train but also a vast, foil-wrapped choccy. Which means 24 chocs in all and not one of them for you.

Plot how to bribe infant next door into returning calendar. Discover only Mother about to deliver same and shamefacedly tell her you have changed mind and wld like to have a calendar for just

34

one more year. Watch sentimental tears form in only mother's peepers. Feel same develop in own peepers when realisation dawns that she has bought you a V.Grown up calendar anyway. No frost, no reindeer, no chocs. Open window number one to reveal picture of glumey pine forest.

Muse on dastardly materialism and ruination of Christmas spirit Etck. NB Days 2-7 in sibling's calendar reveal: two squirrels in Christmas hats, a doll, a ball, a sprig of holly, a rabbit with a parcel and SEVEN CHOCCIES. Muse on unfairness of universe.

TIPS FOR WEEK ONE:
Make a lot of lists.
1 Cards you need to post.
2 Cards you can deliver
3 People you need to buy presents for
4 People you'll make presents for
5 What you'll buy
6 What you'll make

Have long sleep.

z z z z z z z z z z z z z z z z z z z z

WEEK TWO Dec 8-14
On Dec 8th wake to realise that you have failed to act on any of the lists you compiled in week one. You have also failed to learn lines of Christmas song for school

panto, which is V.Radical re-telling of Charles Dickens's *A Christmas Carol* with Scrooge as Evil woodcutter decimating rainforest and Tiny Tim as large female tree symbolising Earth's richness and beauty.

Interesting though the discussions on sizeism, disability and the environment that led up to this new interpretation were, and much as you applauded the spirit of the endeavour Etck. you are feeling somewhat confused by the outcome, as is the Drama teacher, currently off sick with stress.

Oh Gi-ant Forest of the AMAZON

Your song is about the Spirit of Christmas Present bringing new life to the world as long as Scrooge changes his wicked ways. The Spirit of Christmas Future has already appeared, laying waste to Universe Etck with foul pestilences wrought by Evil Humanity, which makes it V Difficult for scene changers to reafforest school stage, hence Yr song must bridge gap while other Teenage Worriers scamper about dressed as redwoods, dismantling nuclear power plants Etck.

You are singing it with five tone deaf frendz and one who has perfect pitch but is currently off sick with Worry. These are the words of your song:

Even Rover's loyalty is stretch

(To tune of "O Little Town of Bethlehem" accompanied by soft patter of rain sounds and fluting, belching and farting noises made by Year Two)

Oh giant forest of the Amazon
How tall we see thee grow
Above thy deep and dreaming sleep
The vi-ile chain-saws go

All ears can hear them coming
But in this world of sin
Unless we all do something now
We canno-ot stop this din.

It will be clear to any self-respecting Teenage Worrier why you find it impossible to remember this, but since it was a collaborative effort no one has the courage to say it is tosh and let's start over. Hence most of staff in state of stress, dread, Etck.

Luckily panto not till Dec 16th, so put off learning lines until Week Three and concentrate on immediate Worries. Decide also to eat some of sibling's left-overs (usually mixed with paint, glue Etck) on Dec 15th in hopes of getting mild case of dysentery on day.

Have Big Worry about how to spread minute savings

How to FAKE Terminal Illness

among vast list of people for whom you feel you need to buy presents. Halve list. Put Father back on list. Halve list again.

What remains shld be immediate family, pets, best frend, lurve object (unless this is Brit-pop star who swore his band wld stay together till end of time and then split up causing you to go into deep mourning for most of last year).

Now you have V.Small list, have little scuffle round bags of oddments, jumble sacks, sibling's dressing-up box Etck to see what you can make some presents out of...

Have big worry about parties and why you haven't been invited to any and what you would wear if you were.

Press nose against toy shop window and wallow in nostalgia re how simple life was when a My Incy Horsey or a Lulu Dolly that Pees and Poos (brilliant device dreamed up by wicked toy manufacturers for inveigling broke parents to cough up for Lulu's nappy supply), or Zsa Zsa Empress of Universe in her Fairy Tale Spaceship were all you needed for perfect happiness. Make mistake of mentioning this to yr Mother, who vents tirade of rage about how you were never happy for more than five mins and always broke hooves, legs, fairy laser rays Etck. within hours of receiving same. Glance at sibling's toys and conclude she was right. Ponder on nature of happiness.

Decide only answer is to be more Spiritual and that you will do small good turn each day and pay seasonal homage to Creator of Universe, birth of whose son we are all supposed to be celebrating Etck. (Maybe this, you schemingly reckon, will clinch the CD Rom computer you yearn for).

Tips for week two

Make cards for nearest and dearest (see El Chubb's designs if short of ideas).

Compile party outfit in case you get invited to anything. This saves panic at last moment and will, in the event of not receiving invites, double for use at scintillating school disco.

Ask only mother (or father, guardian, carer, social worker Etck) what you can do to help, hoping that this eager approach will reassure adult-in-charge of your new, responsible attitude to life so that she is more likely to let you go to any parties that might come up.

Attempt to make list of suitable activities for yawning gap after Christmas. Wish you had kind of family who zipped off for Caribbean tour, or skiing trip. Realise you only know two families like this and one of them belongs to true lurve who has spurned you. Have little cry.

WEEK THREE Dec 14-21 (getting close to BIG DAY)
Dec 14:
Learn Amazon Rainforest song. Sing to family. Retire under hail of abuse, rotten tomatoes, cries of "We're exercising our intellects watching Neighbours" Etck.

Wish, not for first time, that you had kind, supportive family who applauded yr every effort. Realise that yr sibling gets more praise, lurve, patience, attention, presents, fun Etck than you. Sulk.

Dec 15: Only **TEN** Days to go. Arg.

Attempt to contract mild case of food poisoning in order to avoid shambolic panto. Find that concoction you have mixed (making sure not to add anything illegal or lethal – this is a family buke) makes you feel surprisingly well. Cheer up. At least you are not playing Tiny Tim and having to be made up to look like a Tree Goddess.

Have V. Big Worry at large list of tasks that Responsible Adult has given you, including mountains of festive shopping. No party invites yet, so offer to help seems to have backfired.

remains of costume.

Dec 16:

Discover that sibling's gerbil has shredded large portion of yr. Spirit of the Woodland costume. Although yr only mother (responsible adult Etck) in tears at this tragedy, you find that you are feeling strangely cheerful. Was it the dysentery potion, still working its strange magic? Or the slim possibility that you might be excused from panto?

Sadly, latter proves untrue and you are forced to appear, like sore thumb, in borrowed leotard and orange tights while all around are symphonies of viridian and emerald. Only a handful of the audience laughs aloud at the Rain forest song, however (naturally, two of this handful are your own relatives). Most Responsible Adults are in tears of joy at seeing their tiny babas actually on a stage walking, talking and almost singing and dancing. They are remembering their adored offspring at birth, taking first steps Etck and are amazed they have got this far. Their hearts swell at the finale, when Tiny Tim (Tree Goddess) stoops to sweep the reformed wood-cutter Scrooge into her branches, where she cradles him to the strains of a nauseating ditty about Earth's renewal, as First Years scatter flowers over the stage.

Even hard hearted Teenage Worriers, steeped in cynicism, have lumps in throat at this stage, as Drama Teacher, heavily sedated, is wheeled on to accept bouquet. V.Big relief all round as Drama Teacher's speech, instead of being torrent of abuse she has hurled at cast all term, is litany of praise, triumph, stars are born, marvellous team effort Etck Etck. Several parents V.Impressed by simplicity of yr costume, the "wonderful gold" of yr tights having been a "Brilliantly original" tropical touch.

Dec 17:
Glow of triumph re-panto dissolves in glume at realisation that all lists compiled at beginning of month in spirit of good organisation Etck. remain undone. Frantic search for lists reveals they have met same fate as Spirit of Woodland Costume. Resolve never to speak to sibling, or sibling's gerbil, again.

Spend evening re-compiling lists.

Dec 18:

School disco. Wake up worrying about what to wear. Sibling suggests, at breakfast, you wear orange tights, leotard Etck. Maintain haughty silence.

Search frantically through responsible adult's cupboard and find V.Slinky scarlet gown. Beg to wear it. Only Mother says she has never seen it before. Only father looks V.Anxious. Leave to sounds of parents throwing cutlery Etck. Was gown present for only father's floosy? Or is he a Trans-sexual? Worry, worry.

Feel V.Unwell as result of parents' imminent divorce combined with Fashion Worries, pre-Party nerves Etck. Miss disco. Relief followed by sharp regret as wonder who there, who they got off with, whether maths teacher kissing sixth formers under mistletoe Etck. Cry self to sleep.

Dec 19:

Break up. Disco was best ever, everyone can't help telling you. V.Good, sexy Etck. DJ, light show, loads of scandal, Maths teacher sacked for improper conduct Etck. Etck.

Arrange to see Frend to go shopping on 21st. Get three cards (sent 22 at last minute, so V.Bad return on investment).

Wonder if anyone Cares.

Dec 20:

Sleep all day. Decorate room all night.

Dec 21:

Frend fails to meet you at appointed hour to shop. Lose confidence in ability to shop by self. Call on frend who suggests rearranging expedition on Dec 23. Get invitation to party for Dec 22. Panic.

arty outfit Tips ① Get bin bag

WEEK FOUR

② cut into shape

Dec 22:

Spend day making party outfit .Junk outfit at 7pm in favour of jeans and sweatshirt.

Drag reluctant frend to party, hyperventilating all way. Both panic on doorstep and decide not to go in. But door opens and frend is swept inside amid vibrant throng. Hover nervously in hall for two hours.

Summon courage to search for frend. Find her in arms of cleft-chinned wonder-hunk, wearing sparkling reindeer antlers and little else. Retire to kitchen and nibble twiglet. Go home. Wait outside for two hours counting leaves on hedge until frozen. (It would not do to arrive home from only party of the year at 9.30).

③ Throw in bin

Dec 23:

Frend's mum tells you that frend has gone shopping with bloke in antlers, but has promised she will go with you tomorrow.

Sit at home making cards with sibling and throwing oddments on to tree in order to placate haggard mother, who appears to be wrestling with six tons of tin foil. Post cards to relatives. Realise last day for posting has long gone, so write the following missive on each envelope (including the one to your pen-pal in Australia):

"Jolly postman, please be kind
For my old gran will really mind.
If she does not get this card
She will take it really hard.
And who knows, in this time of cheer,
Whether she'll be here next year?"

Nearly miss post as a result. Writhe with guilt and superstition about having lied to postman, especially as you are V.Fond of yr Gran.

Dec 24: CHRISTMAS EVE!

Meet frend. Shop.

At home, realise that things in shopping bag bear no relationship to things on list. Had intended for instance to buy chocs, bubble bath, lots of soap (female relatives), Batman toy (sibling), ear-rings (frend), nice tie (attempt to smarten up only father); flea collar (attempt to smarten up only pet); gerbil poison (joke).

Contents of bag reveal: fur telephone; outsize china mug inscribed "To Diddums from Luvvums"; two books ("How to write a Blockbuster" and "Sibling Rivalry", both reduced and an unmissable bargain at 50p for two); a plastic spice rack (V.V.Cheap); a teddy in a Christmas hat; an oven glove.

Have Big Worry about whether you can change any of these. Since you have lost all receipts, use time creatively to work out how to divide unsuitable presents between lurved ones.

El Chubb's suggestions wld be:

Father......................oven glove
Mother ....china mug (anonymously, to make
                           father jealous)
Grandparent ....How to write a Blockbuster
Sibling ....spice rack (heh, heh)
Pet ....fur telephone
Frend ....teddy

This will leave you free to curl up with "Sibling Rivalry". Heave big sigh of relief and realise it is thought that counts. Help sibling write letter to Santa. Leave out mince pies, saucer of milk Etck. Hang up stocking (hope springs eternal).

    Have little Worry as to whether parent or other responsible adult will notice you bought cheapest crackers with their money (your only contribution to the festive table) and spent change on fudge.

Dec 25 CHRISTMAS DAY
    Your turn to write – Your Diary begins (roll on drums Etck).

N.B. Rover's cracker

December 25 CHRISTMAS DAY

December 26   # BOXING DAY

(Regarded by my lillte
brother Benjy as opportunity
to belt everyone in sight.
EveryTHING, too, as evidenced
   by litter of smashed toys Eeck)

Turkeys breathe out. 364 days of
freedom.

December 27   Day when GLUME
CAN descend.... bear up. You will have
a birthday later in the year (unless
born on Dec 26 or 27 in which case,
condolences. Join a support group).

December 28 **ENJOY** the Holidays!
(not much longer left.)

December 29   Check New Year's Eve
Party Invites. Have little cry.

December 30

Why Not spend a whole day doing a BIG Painting?

Perhaps a MURAL for gr. ickle sibling?

NB. Check with sibling, irresponible adult, Etck before plastering wall with naked HUNKS Etck.

December 31 NEW YEAR'S EVE !

Cry self to sleep at midnight.
Comfort self at thought that
others, too, are lonesome. Resolve to
have party in year 2,000.

January 1 **199.....**

NEW YEAR'S DAY

List resolutions (see if you've kept them by
Jan 2nd)

January 2   Have you kept your resolutions?

January 3   If you have kept yr resolutions
this long, give yourself one star ☆

January 4

January 5

January 6 **TWELFTH NIGHT**

End of Christmas
boo hoo sob.

(Decide not to throw teddy away for ONE
more year, afterall).

☆ ☆ Two stars if any resolutions
kept this long.

JAN continued...

This page is for the rest of
January.... Put in Weather,
Lurve, Frendz, Outings, Food,
Glume Etck. Or use for scrap-book
Etck. Etck.

FEBRUARY

Now, dear reader, I give you two pages for each month of the year. List what you HOPE for (and what happened.....). Or just DOODLE....

FEB part TWO:

MARCH:

MARCH part Two:

APRIL

Easter will be now-ish (if not in
March). Expect snow.

APRIL part TWO:

MAY

Birthday of
L. Chubb.
(will anyone
remember? Sob)

MAY part Two...

JUNE....

Get ready to play tennis.
Decide against it. Watch Wimbledon
instead.

JUNE continued....

JULY...

SUZY continued ♣♣♣

Slim possibility of weekend in
Frinton....

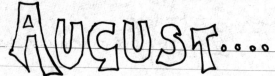 AUGUST....

V. Bad sunburn as result
of weekend in Frinton. Luckily,
Aug v. wet. Hayfever bad, even so.

AUG part two.....

September....

Sept ..CONTINUED ooooo

OCTOBER....

OCT part Two.............

NOVEMBER...

Burn nose on sparkler. Since
v. red due to cold, not much
difference.

NOV.. continued......

Take pets to vet re- firework
psychosis.

DECEMBER..

Er... have we been here
before? Does nothing change?

DEC continued......

Christmas certainly on Dec 25.

and back to JANUARY
again ....

(if any resolutions kept from last
year, award self 200 stars &
send for Teenage Worrier's Scroll
of Honour, available from EC Chubb
Products at only £52.90p t p&p).

Jan cont:
   Remember to buy new
diary by Letty Chubb...
(ahem).

EL CHUBB'S GUIDE TO CHRISTMAS HOLIDAY ACTIVITIES.

HOW TO PLAY IN SNOW

Recapture lost youth (unless he is in arms of best frend, Etck) by cavorting in soft swathes of pristine crystals – a veritable marshmallow of delights, just like in Raymond Briggs's The Snowman. Snow, as you know, always falls softly on Dec 23 covering the little churches, fields Etck with a merry frosting through which robins, holly Etck merrily sing, postpeople wheel bicycles and children cheerily sledge, cavort, Etck.

Teenage Worriers who live in countryside, Scotland Etck are often lucky enough to witness scenes such as these. Southern Urban Worriers however are more likely to curse at sight of grey sludge under fine layer of grit which follows first pattering of snowfall, in the unlikely event of getting any snow at all before Easter.

If lucky enough to have snow (NB if you are bored by snow you are too old for this buke and shld be hiring your retirement home already) you may enjoy a few of the following ideas;

1 RADICAL!

Build a snow woman. Feminist Teenage Worriers often lament the lack of these elegant creatures in the snow season. An attempt to build one, however, soon demonstrates reason for lack of same. Building snow bazooms is almost as difficult as building real ones, but it is cheering to reflect that real ones do not slide to ground with soft plopping sound (one potential worry crossed off list). I have tried filling a wonder bra with snow but it looked V.Rude. So I have relented and re-named all snow sculptures "snow persons".

2 SNOWBALL FIGHT

In which you get V.V. large pile of snowballs ready and then innocently ask boy/gurl of yr Dreamz for frosty walk. He/She will be amazed by the speed and dexterity with which you have formed snowballs (carefully concealed in large freezer box inside yr coat) and join in with merry abandon until you are both rolling sensuously in snow drift. Lurve object will be amazed by your slenderness (as you will have by now divested yourself of freezer box) and, anxious to be a good sport, will challenge you to another fight tomorrow. Phew. Stay up all night making snowballs to store

85

in freezer. Sadly, freezer compartment in our fridge is only big enough for one and a half packs of fish fingers......

3 SLEDGING

Although the Ski-Wynterson family three doors down have skates, skis and assorted sledges for several different kinds of snow, I have always been too proud to ask to borrow any of them and have preferred a tin tray to pull Benjy along on, during the few rare snowfalls of his existence to date. He falls off a tin tray at least as fast as the Ski-Wynterson children fall off their posh wooden sledges with bells on and I feel it gives us street cred. Also, if I push him hard enough, he usually yells V.Loud – an incentive for a cleft chinned wunderbabe to emerge, sweep him up and tenderly ask if that magnificent snow queen yonder (moi, naturellement) is his big sister? Hot chocolate and canoodling follows this scenario time after time (or it would if I was a snow queen and there were any cleft-chinned wunder hunks within five mile zone Etck).

HORRORSCOPES

MAKE UP YOUR OWN PREDICTIONS FOR NEXT YEAR

These are the predictions of El Chubb and will do just as well as any you can read in Teenybop, Yoo-Hoo, Tru-Luv, Smirk Etck.

I am prepared to believe there are some V Serious and even some V Good astrologers Out There, who spend many hours working out charts based on V. Accurate info Etck. But if you think that Madame Boo Boo Von Haddock, who writes for Teeny-weeny Weekly has given this much attention to yr own personal life, then ask yourself why all the other Taureans you know are V. Happy while you are sunk in glume?

Now for El Chubb's Unique Horoscope guide to next Year:

Let us, for a moment, imagine you are a vulnerable Teenage Worrier, anxious to know what the new year has in store for you. So you buy El Chubbo's guide to the year, pausing only to check that El Chubbo (pictured in diaphanous robes on front of book, gazing into crystal ball Etck) is a great grand-daughter of Gipsy Rose Lee, has a Romany-look ear-ring, V.Large soulful eyes that look as though they know the Secrets of your Soul and has washed her face in dew each midsummer's night. You turn, feverishly, to your sign (let us imagine you are Capricorn) and read on...

EL CHUBBO

PREDICTS YOUR FUTURE

88

Capricorn

Jan:

You are certain to get out of bed sometime this month (unless suffering from a severe illness or disability) but you may find, when you do, that you are a little cold. Your highest expectations may not be met, but there will be compensations.

Feb:

You will meet someone you really like.

March:

You will meet someone ELSE who is VV Nice.

April:

You will have a disappointment but also a pleasant surprise.

May:

Do not be upset by a disagreement, for you will find what you are searching for!

June:

You may find you are working harder than you like, but you will reap the rewards later.

July:

You deserve a break, be kind to yourself.

August:

On one or two days this month, Capricorns may feel uncomfortably warm. You may cross water. Be careful not to eat anything that disagrees with you.

September:

You will meet someone rather unusual.

October:

Be dashing! Something new to wear is in the offing!

November:

You will hear loud noises and see beautiful but strange colours. However all is well.

December:

You may feel you are getting less than your due. You will see trees covered in lights.

N.B. <u>Diet tip</u>: Capricorns, being Goats, could, and should, eat old gloves.

<u>N.N.B.</u> This tip is as accurate as above predictions.........

The nervous Capricorn, on reading this, will feel swoops of highs and lows:

Although a leeetle depressed by predictions for Jan (their highest expectations may have centred on their birthday, which, being so V.Near Christmas, never brings as many presents as they hoped), Capricorn's heart will soar at the prospect of Feb (could this be Lurve?) and leap even higher for the VV Nice person in March.

In April a harsh note of realism is struck, only to be illumined by a hint of more hope... Fulfillment in May! June brings drudgery but it's worth it! Self-congratulation for July. August cld be better, but WHO is this unusual being you meet in September??? October – goodness me, is the unusual person buying you CLOTHES? Clearly you will have mystical experiences in November (probably as a result of meeting unusual person in Sept). In December, these experiences obviously continue —what an exciting year. This is what El Chubbo Wants you to think, dear, gullible Reader.

BUT.......

Any discerning Teenage Worrier can see some, er, gaps in these predictions. Frinstance: "You will meet someone who is VV Nice".

This cld be your gran, your sibling's friend's mum, the newsagent Etck Etck. You are bound to meet nice people all the time.

Let us take another eg at random: "You will find what you are searching for!" This cld be yr socks (fat chance in case of moi), the cornflakes Etck. Now look again at June's prediction. This is exam month, therefore almost certain to contain a teensy bit of work. Or August: You are bound to cross water, either by going on hols or stepping over puddle in bathroom. You will be certain to be slightly warm at some time in Aug, unless, contrary to predictions of Global-Warming Jeremias, a second ice-age is coming. And in September you meet someone rather unusual. Perhaps it's that nice old unicyclist down the road who juggles with bananas? Or the only person in the neighbourhood with a job? And what new clothes are you likely to get in October? Probably gloves, as last year's pair will have been lost. Or maybe a scarf. If you are lucky enough to have a knitting grandparent (as opposed to a grandparent with nits) you may even get a matching bolero and bobble hat (next year's colours, El Chubbo can predict with confidence, will be vermilion and tangerine)...November's mystical experiences are likely to be the result of a municipal Guy Fawkes display. December's are doubtless Christmas decorations. Also, Capricorns always feel they have got slightly less than their due in either Dec or Jan as their birthdays are V near Christmas and therefore they never get enough presents (see also Jan, above).

But let me not turn you into a total cynic, dearest reader. Write down your predictions for each month here and see if they come true. Do one set for you and one set for the planet. If you are more than 50% accurate, you cld get a v. well paid job as an astrologer (or you could always offer to guess the sex of pregnant women's babies – if you always say "gurl" you are bound to be right at least half the time).

I, Chubb
will
GUESS THE
SEX OF YOUR
BABY
(Money back
if wrong)

Heh! Heh! Even the wrong ones probably won't bother to claim their money back...

Here are some things to consider for world predictions, in case you are short of ideas.

BAD THINGS:

Famine; Plague; Mad Cow Disease across Europe; Earthquakes, serial killings, mass slaughter, bombings, wars, all usual stuff Etck.

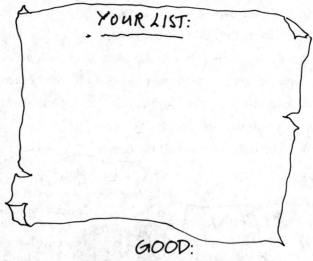

YOUR LIST:

GOOD:

Mad cow disease causes world to grow soya beans; Micro-chip invented that grows enough soya beans to feed entire world; Product patented (by El Chubb, we hope) that makes soya beans taste exactly like fillet steak (also saves lives of all cows and creates new planet where they can live at peace, somewhere just above moon); Virus manufactured by computer nerd (El Chubb in disguise) that disables weapons, enabling them only to fire porridge. Scotland becomes foremost nation in world as result of huge increase in demand for porridge oats. Kilts become obligatory dress for human male who wants to Get On.

World peace endures for a thousand years, interrupted only by occasional splats of porridge from a handful of crazed militia men holed up in the Andes and attempting to reinvent nuclear weapons (which, since new virus, can only emit small fart-like explosions reminiscent of bran flakes). No cereal killer jokes, please.

YOUR LIST:

Good Deeds Time

Why not

1.
Give your darling parent (social worker, carer, irresponsible adult, Etck) a Meal Off?
This means doing some cooking.

Recipe below serves one:
Open can.
Put slice of bread in toaster.
Pour contents of can into saucepan.
Turn on cooker ring and or light gas.
Place saucepan on gas.
Listen for distinctive popping
noise of toast coming out of toaster.

<u>NB.</u> <u>Tip</u>: A watched toaster never pops

Investigate lack of popping noise and discern burning smell of toast stuck in toaster.

Bang toaster.
Scrape thick layer of charcoal off toast.
Hunt for butter/spread.
Hunt for plate.

(No clean plates available in our house so I usually use a paper tissue – preferably clean)

Scrape top layer of beans off underlying (burnt) layer of beans.

Wonder why beans look such strange colour, and rather large.

Realise it was not can of beans after all, but tin of apricots in syrup.
Decide this will be V.original meal.
Place warm apricots on toast.
Throw away saucepan to cover tracks.
Place toast on plate. (or tissue)

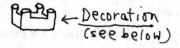 ← Decoration (see below)

Decorate with sprig of parsley (if no parsley a little bit of grass or green Lego will do).

2.

Give adult a treat by making their bed?

Find items in bed you wish you had not known about and decide on other good deed, knowing you will never feel quite the same about adult again and that another piece of yr precious childhood has been ripped untimely from you.

CENSORED

← My publisher has forbidder my portrait of said items on grounds of decenc

3.

Take complete charge of pet for whole holidays.

(El Chubb's advice is only to do this if yours is a goldfish whose tank has just been cleaned – even the V.V.V.Laziest teenage Worrier can find the strength to scatter a few fingerfuls of fish food once every two days.)

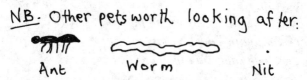

NB. Other pets worth looking after:

Ant   Worm   Nit

4. Tidy yr room.

Although disguised as good deed (because bound to give yr parent a glow of pride that lasts for a whole day – I am being realistic about how long your room will STAY tidy – this is beneficial to a Teenage Worrier, also. Viz: V.Quick to find things. V. Nice not to trip over bag of chips Etck. Think of the hours in Casualty you can save. V. Exciting, too, to come across old mementoes Etck that you now want to stick pins into, weep over Etck.

NB If you share room with sibling, make sure they do their half. If they refuse, take care to pick up everything that is theirs and put it IN (not on) their bed. Although it will take a couple more minutes to make their bed look a little bit neat by smoothing duvet over their mouldy toys, the rewards, in terms of gloating satisfaction, will be great. Specially true if they are apt to leave hlf-full cans of Coke lying about. For true satisfaction to be obtained, sibling must be warned of this. Otherwise they will run screaming to parent (if younger) or run screaming at you (if older). Neither event has happy consequences.

TIPS FOR QUICK TIDY.

Get V. Big box.

Put every single thing except furniture, light,

teddy, a couple of books, your diary in box.

Shove box under bed.

If box too big, cover with cloth and use as table.

This shld take one minute ten seconds.

(Er, it took a little longer in the case of MOI – as I sadly became sentimental and stopped to read my primary school books Etck).

Sort through box whenever you want anything.

5.

Offer to mow lawn.

V. Good time of year to offer this kind of help, as lawn does not grow till spring. If no garden, as in sad case of moi, offer to weed, water window box (one minute) or sweep yard (an arduous two minutes including finding broom).

After weeding window box relax in same (as long as not tower block dweller.)

6.
Do some shopping.

Sample list from parent:
(With EXACTLY right money, calculated
down to last penny)

Loo paper
cleaning stuff
fish fingers
baked beans
sprouts
gourmet olive oil
   (attempt to give fake gourmet
   flavour to sprouts)
b.beans
f.fingers

Q: What is this?

Teen Worrier returns with:

Loo paper
cleaning stuff
fish fingers
baked beans
sprouts
V.cheap veggie oil (which she pours into
   old gourmet olive oil bottle)
FUDGE

A: Fish fingers, what else?

THINK OF OTHER NICE THINGS
YOU CAN DO FOR OTHERS:
(v. little space):

AND FOR YOURSELF:
(v. Big space):

O

O

ARE YOU A TRUE
NEW YEAR WORRIER?

Are you worried about any of the following?

(Tick appropriate box)

1 Whether you will live till next Christmas?

2 Whether lurved ones will live till next Christmas?

3 Whether world will survive till next Christmas?

4 Whether you should make New Year Resolutions in case you, lurved ones, planet Etck don't survive the year?

5 Whether singing "Hey diddle diddle the cat and the fiddle" to your sibling will give you Mad Cow Disease?

6 Whether the sky will fall on your head if you leave one Christmas decoration up by mistake after Jan 6?

7 Whether you will get as far as Easter without a cold sore?

8 Whether you shld send a New Year card to the person of your Dreamz?

	VVV Worried	VV Worried	V Worried	Worried	not Worried	HAPPY about
1	☐	☐	☐	☐	☐	☐
2	☐	☐	☐	☐	☐	☐
3	☐	☐	☐	☐	☐	☐
4	☐	☐	☐	☐	☐	☐
5	☐	☐	☐	☐	☐	☐
6	☐	☐	☐	☐	☐	☐
7	☐	☐	☐	☐	☐	☐
8	☐	☐	☐	☐	☐	☐

9 Whether you will be asked to any parties before next Christmas?

10 Whether to go if you are asked?

11 Whether you will enjoy Christmas next year, or will you be too old for fun by then?

12 Whether you'll ever have sex?

13 Whether you'll get a single GCSE?

14 Whether you'll get a job when you leave school?

15 Or ever?

16 Whether pets have souls?

17 Whether people have souls?

18 How to be a Better Person?

19 Whether you will ever learn to roller blade?

20 Whether your pet will ever learn to roller blade?

	VVV Worried	VV Worried	V Worried	Worried	not Worried	HAPPY about
9	☐	☐	☐	☐	☐	☐
10	☐	☐	☐	☐	☐	☐
11	☐	☐	☐	☐	☐	☐
12	☐	☐	☐	☐	☐	☐
13	☐	☐	☐	☐	☐	☐
14	☐	☐	☐	☐	☐	☐
15	☐	☐	☐	☐	☐	☐
16	☐	☐	☐	☐	☐	☐
17	☐	☐	☐	☐	☐	☐
18	☐	☐	☐	☐	☐	☐
19	☐	☐	☐	☐	☐	☐
20	☐	☐	☐	☐	☐	☐

See answers P. 22 which V. cleverly
and scientifickly apply to both Quizzes.

GAMES TO PLAY DURING THOSE LONG WINTER DAYZ AND NIGHTZ

HEADS BODIES & TAILS

Best with three people, but quite fun with two, even if one of them is only five (as in case of moi and Benjy). Each person has sheet of paper plus pencil.

Everyone draws a head on their sheet (making sure no one else can see) then folds it back and hands it on to the next person who draws the body, leaving two lines for legs, then hands it on to next person (or back to first person) who draws legs and feet.

V.Funny results.

Teenage Worrier's variation wld be to cut out heads of manky Brit-pop stars, super-models Etck, paste them on paper, shuffle, fold over and draw bodies for them. My favourite was Brad Pitbull with a vast cleavage (from v.seedy mag I found in my father's drawer) and horse's legs (see diagram).

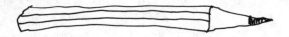

108

NB. A Head body & Tail by BENJY + Frend age 6.

STANDING ON THE CHAIR GAME

One person has to stand on chair in front of everyone else. They are given something to say (it could be just "Strawberry jam" or "Because I am a pumpkin") and they are only allowed to say these words in response to the cruel questions they will be asked by the revolting throng that surrounds them.

They are not allowed to laugh. Once they do, they are off the chair and it is someone else's turn to be humiliated. People laugh V.Quickly during this game usually, even when they are told to say something V.Inoffensive like "Yes, it is a pleasant day". This is one of those mysteries of human nature that L.Chubb often ponders in the small dark hours. This game should only be played with people you know V.Well, unless you like being slowly tortured.

N.B. My attempt to make this game more exciting (ahem) ended badly.

Do not try this at home...

GLUMEY FAMILIES

V. Like traditional "Happy Families" card game, but using L. Chubb's pack (see below) which shld be marketed soon by El Chubb Enterprises Ltd. The object of the game is to split up as many families as possible. I am working out the fine tuning of the rules at the moment........

Mr Cadaver the undertaker

Mrs Morgue the Taxidermist

Master Snot the Lottery Winner's son

Miss Abyss the Bank Manager's daughter

Mr Meek the bailiff's husband

Mrs Grabbit the Lawyer's wife.

N.B. Small sprinkling of six designs so far... please send yours to Moi, Letty Chubb (see address at back of buke).

EL CHUBB'S CROSSWORD

(made up entirely of Cross words)

Or GLUMEY
words

(maybe
I'll do

HAPP
WOR
nex
(Tra
la
joy
Fun
Etc

Clues

Across

1. Saddest word in world (when spoken by yr. beLurred)
3. Crazy ride
5. L. Chubb's feeling while compiling this Crossword
6. Expression of disgust.
7. Dishevelled gear leads to anger

Down

1. See 1 Across
2. Snow White might have felt a little ------
3. Rhymes with 5 Across
4. Very like jerks, but more daft
5. A dog's expletive

A aargh... answers on p. 116 (I think I'll stick to knitting)

THE NEW YEAR'S RESOLUTION GAME

In which you make V.Wise, socially acceptable resolutions on Jan 1st and see how long you can keep them when temptation rears ugly mug.

Since object is to get to end of game first with as many resolutions intact as poss., temptation to break resolutions is great. Worth remembering then, that person who gets to end first does not always win (so true of Life itself Etck). Problem is, players may die of boredom (or boardom, as we board game inventors call it) while V.Careful player minces around keeping all their resolutions by not setting foot outside Etck (Also V. True of real life, although it's surprising how many resolutions you can break just sitting at home in lonely room pining).

DO NOT
USE GLASSES,
MUGS, CUPS
or BOTTLES

esolution: No Alcohol

DO NOT
Put paper in
yr. mouth

Resolution: No fags

DO NOT
Have any
POSSESSIONS

solution: Keep tidy

DO NOT
GO TO BED

Resolution: Be up
Early

mples of cards used in this game.
esolve to make up your own.

SWAPPING

After Christpud, v.many Teenage Worriers find a certain lethargy overcomes them. They already had too many things in their room and now they've got even more. Most of them are not things they are V.fond of...SO, SWAP. Get your frend (or frendz, if you are lucky enough to have more than one, sob) to bring round their most unwanted Christmas presents Etck and swap their V.Nice CD-Roms for your Bunty Annual Etck (if only life were really like this). This is also V.Fun to do with clothes...BUT (I always like to use a big but now and then) do not, even though temptation be V.Strong, swap the orange and purple (or lemon and turquoise, or puce and emerald) bolero your Granny knitted. Not even for a back-of-the-lorryload of Armani Etck. You will only regret it when you see your Granny sobbing. Same goes for pencil case glued out of felt by sibling. There are some things (not many, I know) worth more than mere money.

← Benjy wants this back

small cactus

Ball of string

sadly, these were only things I had to swap. No one wanted them.

Wooooo o o ooooooh!

PSYCHIC CHUBB

Wooooooooo ooh!

You can convince your frendz you are psychic by the following scam:

First get four scraps of paper. Without your frend seeing, write "red" on one, "blue" on the next, "carrot" on the third, "cabbage" on the fourth. Place them under a plate, in your pocket, or anywhere where you will know what each one is.

Then ask your frend to reply immediately to the following questions:

"Think of a colour"

"Think of a vegetable"

NB V. imp. that they reply V. Quickly.

Nearly everyone says either red or blue, and carrot or cabbage.

At this point you whisk out piece of paper on which you have written said colour or veggie to admiring gasps from selected throng.

NB. This is no more of a con than most 'PSYCHICS'.

Now, to prove I am Psychic:

Your past: You have read the word 'psychic' (or, um, tried to...)

Your present: You are reading this now.

Your Future: You will stop holding this book.

115

Answers to L.Chubb's
CROSSWORD.

Across

1. No
3. Dire
5. Gloom
6. Yuk
7. Rage

Down

1. No
2. Grumpy
3. Doom
4. Berks
5. Grrr

Shade in dotted areas. If you prefer
Pic A you are over 16. If B, under 16.
(er... perhaps... um, with some exceptions)

Invent your own games
here:

Please send to L. Chubb C/o
Piccadilly Press, 5 Castle Rd
LONDON NW1 8PR.
(so I can get v. rich)

Name:
Address:

Tel:
_____

Name:
Address:

Tel:
_____

Name:
Address:

Tel:
_____

Name:
Address:

Tel:
_____

Name:
Address:

Tel: _____

Name:
Address:

Tel: _____

Name:
Address:

Tel: _____

Name:
Address:

Tel: _____

Name:
Address:

Tel: _____

Name:
Address:

Tel: _____

Name:
Address:

Tel: _____

Name:
Address:

Tel: _____

Name:
Address:

Tel:

Name:
Address:

Tel:

Name:
Address:

Tel:

Name:
Address:

Tel:

NOTES

NOTES

NOTES

Ta Ta
For now

N.B. 'The Teenage
Worrier's Guide
to LIFE' out soon!

Dear Letty

    I _ _ _ _ _ _ _ _ _ your book.
Could you please write about
and . . . .
  This is what I got for
Christmas: . . . .
. . . .

This is what I wanted:
. . . .

I am . . . . . years old.

from

P.S . . . .
. . . .
. . . .

If you can be bothered, send
this page to: Letty Chubb,
C/o Piccadilly Press,
    5 Castle Rd,
LONDON NW1 8PR.
        Thanks! Bye!
          xx Letty